# SUN UP

*Mornin' Vittles*

*Breakfast*

## Sourdough Starter

A good starter was one of the most precious possessions on the ranch or the trail. Cooks were known to sleep with the starter on cold nights to keep it alive. Using commercial yeast to make the starter is a short cut. In the old days, cooks made their own yeast with a batter of flour, potato water, salt, sugar and yeast cells from the air to furnish the enzymes. This was a tricky process and explains why a good starter was so valuable.

| | |
|---|---|
| 1 | package active dry yeast |
| 1/4 | cup lukewarm water (potato water is good) |
| 2 | cups warm water |
| 1-1/2 | cups flour |
| 1 | tablespoon sugar |

Using a quart size fruit jar or crock, dissolve yeast with 1/4 cup water. Allow to stand several minutes then stir in water, flour and sugar. Cover with a cloth. Leave overnight at room temperature. Stir down several times as mixture rises to top.

The longer the mixture stands at room temperature, the stronger the sour taste. Replace cover and refrigerate until ready to use. To maintain an ample supply of starter, each time you use it, replenish it with equal amounts of warm water and flour. Makes about 2 cups.

# Sourdough Biscuits

*A chuck wagon staple.*

Mix the night before using:

| | |
|---|---|
| 1 | cup sourdough starter, at room temperature |
| 1/2 | cup warm water |
| 1 | cup all-purpose flour |

Let stand overnight at room temperature. About 1 hour before serving, turn dough out 1 cup of the flour on a bread board. Combine remaining 1/2 cup flour with baking powder, soda, salt and sugar.

| | |
|---|---|
| 1-1/2 | cups flour |
| 2 | teaspoons baking powder |
| 1/2 | teaspoon baking soda |
| 1/2 | teaspoon salt |
| 1 | tablespoon sugar |
| | Bacon drippings or butter |

Knead flour lightly into batter. Make a well in the dough and mix dry ingredients into the batter, kneading lightly to get correct consistency for rolling dough without sticking. Roll to 1/2 inch thickness. Cut biscuits with a cutter or into 2"x3" rectangles. Brush tops with warm bacon drippings; or warm butter. Place biscuits 1/2 inch apart on baking sheet, or close together in a 9 inch square pan, and set in a warm place to rise about 1/2 hour. Bake at 400 degrees about 20 minutes. For outdoor cooking, place biscuits in a cast iron skillet, cover with foil and place on grill 3" from hot coals. After 10 minutes, lift foil to be sure biscuits are not burning. Cook 5 minutes longer or until done. Makes 14 biscuits.

# Biscuits on a Stick

Cowboys on the range cooking for themselves used green wood sticks to cook chunks of meat and biscuits over a campfire. Sodium Bicarbonate [baking soda] was commercially produced in America from 1846. After that time, a cowboy's provisions usually included a sack of flour, a little salt, baking soda, bacon, lard and coffee. With a little liquid, approximately 1/3 cup liquid to 1 cup flour with a hunk of lard cut in, he could mix up a biscuit dough, wrap it around a stick and hold it over a fire until cooked.

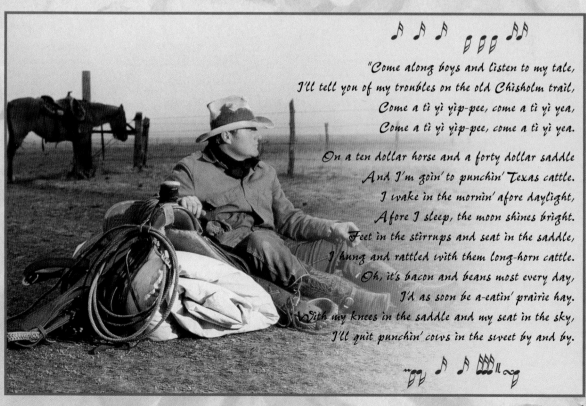

"Come along boys and listen to my tale,
I'll tell you of my troubles on the old Chisholm trail,
Come a ti yi yip-pee, come a ti yi yea,
Come a ti yi yip-pee, come a ti yi yea.

On a ten dollar horse and a forty dollar saddle
And I'm goin' to punchin' Texas cattle.
I wake in the mornin' afore daylight,
Afore I sleep, the moon shines bright.
Feet in the stirrups and seat in the saddle,
I hung and rattled with them long-horn cattle.
Oh, it's bacon and beans most every day,
I'd as soon be a-eatin' prairie hay.
With my knees in the saddle and my seat in the sky,
I'll quit punchin' cows in the sweet by and by.

# Roundup Breakfast

*These mighty good vittles, made in the more permanent camps of the roundups, where food supplies were not so far away, would get them cowboys up and ready to ride at first light.*

| | |
|---|---|
| 2 | pounds country sausage |
| 4 | potatoes, peeled and diced into 1/2 inch cubes |
| 12 | eggs, beaten |
| 1/4 | cup water or milk |

Brown sausage in large skillet. Remove sausage. Heat the pan drippings to medium high; add potatoes and fry, stirring occasionally, about 10 minutes, until browned and partially cooked. Stir potatoes to make a level layer at bottom of skillet, then add sausage on top. In a separate dish, add water or milk to eggs and beat thoroughly. Pour eggs over sausage evenly. Cover and cook over medium heat until eggs are set, about 25 minutes. Serves 6 to 8.

# Dog Kelly's Favorite Griddle Cakes

| | |
|---|---|
| 8 | slices bacon, cut in half and cooked |
| 2 | cups flour |
| 2 | tablespoons baking powder |
| 3 | tablespoons sugar |
| 1/2 | teaspoon salt |
| 2 | eggs, beaten |
| 1-1/2 | cups milk |
| 3 | tablespoons oil or bacon drippings |

Combine dry ingredients, add eggs and milk. Cook bacon until done but not dry. Move bacon aside to accommodate griddle cakes. Using a half slice of bacon for each cake, pour batter over bacon onto hot griddle. Turn the cakes when they begin to look dry around the edges. Cakes should be light, tender and golden brown in color. Serve hot, directly from griddle to plate. Serve with syrup, honey or preserves, if desired. Makes 16 cakes.

# Sourdough Pancakes

Mix the night before using:

| | |
|---|---|
| 2 | cups flour |
| 2 | cups milk |
| 1 | cup starter |

Let stand overnight at room temperature.

When ready to bake, add:

| | |
|---|---|
| 2 | eggs, beaten |
| 1 | teaspoon baking soda |
| 1 | teaspoon salt |

Stir batter until well mixed. Grease griddle if necessary. Pour or spoon pancake batter onto hot griddle. When bubbly and puffed, turn and brown other side. Serve with your favorite syrup. Makes 16 pancakes.

For future use, add:

| | |
|---|---|
| 1 | cup water to original jar |
| 1 | cup flour |
| 1 | tablespoon sugar |

Keep refrigerated.

# Gunslinger's Scrapple

| | |
|---|---|
| 1/2 | pound ground beef or pork or mixture of both |
| 1 | teaspoon salt |
| 1/8 | teaspoon pepper |
| 1 | cup cornmeal |
| 1 | medium onion, chopped |
| 1-1/4 | cups water |

Brown meat and onion slowly in a little fat. Add seasonings and water. Cook over low heat 20 minutes. Add the cornmeal and cook for 45 minutes. Turn into a mold, cool, cut into slices and fry in hot fat until brown. Serve with gravy. Serves 6.

# Alhambra Saloon's Coffee Cake

| | |
|---|---|
| 1/4 | cup butter |
| 1/2 | cup sugar |
| 1 | egg, beaten |
| 1 1/2 | cups flour |
| 2 | teaspoons baking powder |
| 1/2 | teaspoon salt |
| 1/2 | cup milk |
| 1 | egg yolk, slightly beaten |
| 2 | tablespoons cream |

## Sugar Crumb Topping:

| | |
|---|---|
| 1/2 | cup brown sugar |
| 3 | tablespoons flour |
| 1 | teaspoon cinnamon |
| 3 | tablespoons butter |
| 1/2 | cup chopped nuts |

Cream butter and sugar until light, add egg and beat well. Add dry ingredients alternately with milk, blending well after each addition. Turn into greased and floured 9 inch square pan. Blend egg yolk and cream together and pour over top of batter. Make the topping by mixing all ingredients together into a crumbly mixture. Sprinkle over surface of cake. Bake in a preheated 375 degree oven for about 30 minutes. Serve warm. Serves 8.

# Bonanza Brunch Egg Casserole

| | |
|---|---|
| 1 | pound sausage, cooked and drained |
| 4 | large onions, diced |
| 12 | slices white bread, quartered |
| 3 | cups grated Cheddar cheese |
| 8 | eggs, beaten |
| 4 | cups milk |
| 1/4 | teaspoon pepper |
| 1/2 | teaspoon dry mustard |

Saute onion in sausage drippings until soft. Place 1/2 of the bread in the bottom of a greased 9 X 13 inch pan. Sprinkle 1/2 of sausage, onions and cheese on bread; repeat these layers. Combine eggs, milk and spices; pour over top layer. Refrigerate for at least 24 hours before cooking. Remove from refrigerator one hour before serving. Bake at 350 degrees for 45 to 50 minutes. Serves 10.

A cowboy working out on the range, often alone, ate a limited variety of food, usually what he could carry in his canvas saddle bags: Salted beef, pork, bacon, beans and biscuits along with a small supply of corn meal, lard, baking soda, coffee, salt and sugar. Every cowboy eagerly anticipated the exhausting bedlam of the roundup, where a good cook, more than anyone else, was the key to a good roundup. A chuck wagon cook used large pots and Dutch ovens over open fires to feed 30 or 40 men three meals a day, then moved on to a new roundup site before nightfall. Staple fare was pinto beans, bacon, biscuits and SOB stew (stewed entrails). Special treats included gingerbread, rice pudding, bread pudding, cobblers and fruit pies. The cowboys enjoyed these desserts with scalding cups of coffee while squatting around the campsite swapping tall tales.

# Trail Drive Milk Gravy

| 3 | tablespoons bacon fat OR |
|---|---|
| | other meat drippings |
| 3 | tablespoons flour |
| 1 | 12 ounce can evaporated milk |
| 1/2 | cup water |
| | Salt and freshly ground pepper |

In a large skillet, heat the drippings over medium heat. Stir in flour and cook about 1 minute until flour begins to brown. Gradually add the milk and water, stirring until thickened. Season with salt and pepper. Serve over biscuits, bread, steaks or chicken. Makes 1-1/2 cups gravy.

# Johnnycake

| 1 | cup white cornmeal |
|---|---|
| 1 | teaspoon salt |
| 2 | cups scalded milk or water |
| 2 | tablespoons molasses (optional) |
| | Butter (optional) |

Mix cornmeal and salt. Gradually stir in milk or water and molasses, if used. Spread batter 1/4 inch deep in a greased shallow pan or skillet. If desired, dot with small bits of butter. Bake in a hot oven about 20 minutes until crisp. Yields 6 servings.

"Out where the handclasp's a little stronger,
Out where the smile dwells a little longer,
That's where the West begins.

Out where the skies are a trifle bluer,
Out where friendship's a little truer.
Where there's more of singing and
        less of sighing,
Where there's more of giving and less of buying,
And a man makes friends without half trying,
........That's where the West begins."

From "Out Where the West Begins",
Stanzas 1-3, by Arthur Chapman.

# Jake's Buttermilk Doughnuts

| 4-1/2 | cups flour |
|---|---|
| 1/4 | teaspoon nutmeg |
| 1/4 | teaspoon allspice |
| 1-1/2 | teaspoons baking soda |
| 1-1/2 | teaspoons cream of tarter |
| 1 | teaspoon salt |
| 3 | eggs |
| 1 | cup sugar |
| 3 | tablespoons shortening, melted |
| 1 | cup buttermilk |
| | Oil for deep-frying |

Mix together thoroughly the dry ingredients, except the sugar. Beat the eggs until thick and gradually add the sugar. Add the melted shortening, buttermilk and flour mixture to the beaten sugar and egg mixture. Mix well; chill for 1 hour. Turn out onto floured board. Roll to 1/2 inch thickness, cut with floured doughnut cutter. Heat fat to 375° and fry a few at a time in fat that has been heated to 375 degrees until golden brown on both sides, turning once. Drain on paper towels. Dust with confectioners' sugar. Makes about 2 1/2 dozen.

*Chuck Wagon, Rolling Kitchen.*

## Chuck Wagon Pinto Beans

*Dried beans were a staple on the trail. Sometimes the cookie varied the standard onion-and-chile- flavored beans with a little bit of sweetening.*

| | |
|---|---|
| 1 | pound pinto beans |
| 8 | cups water |
| 1 | ham hock OR 1/2 cup salt pork, diced |
| 1 | pound tomatoes, crushed OR 2 cups canned tomatoes |
| 1/2 | cup brown sugar OR honey |
| | Salt and pepper to taste |

Pick over beans, cover with water and soak overnight. The next day, drain the beans and place in a large heavy kettle with a lid. Add 8 cups fresh water, the salt pork and the tomato sauce. Place the beans over a medium-high fire and bring to a steady simmer. Cook steadily 1 hour, then add brown sugar and additional hot water to maintain the water level about 2 inches above the beans. Cook another hour or two, adding hot water as necessary. Add salt to taste. Serves 6 to 8.

## The Chuck Wagon

The chuck wagon was the rolling kitchen for the cowboys trailing herds north from Texas or for round-up crews on cattle ranches. The best wagon design is credited to Charles Goodnight who rebuilt a surplus Army wagon which had extra-durable iron axles and to which he attached a cubbyhole box with drawers at the back of the wagon facing the rear with a hinged lid that let down with a swinging leg to form a work table.

Other customary accessories included a large water barrel, a tool box and a canvas canopy cover. The wagon carried all the cook's bulk supplies of food, pots, pans, skillets, utensils and first aid supplies, as well as the cowboys' bedrolls and personal gear. Wagon manufacturers, including the Studebaker Company, began producing chuck wagons commercially and sold them for about $100.

# Wagon Cook's Root Vegetable Hash

| | |
|---|---|
| 1 | tablespoon butter |
| 2 | tablespoons olive oil, divided |
| 1 | cup onions, chopped |
| 2 | garlic cloves, crushed |
| 1/2 | cup leeks, chopped |
| 1 | pound celery, sliced |
| 2 | pounds rutabaga, peeled and chopped |
| 1 | pound parsnips, peeled and diced |
| 1 | pound turnips, peeled and chopped |
| 2 | cups chicken broth |
| 1 | teaspoon salt |
| 2 | teaspoons freshly ground pepper |
| 2 | sprigs fresh parsley, chopped |

In a Dutch oven over medium heat, melt butter and half of olive oil. Saute onions, garlic and leeks until softened. Stir in remaining vegetables. Cook 5 minutes. Add chicken broth. Reduce heat to low. Cover and simmer about 30 minutes until vegetables are tender. Can be made ahead to this point and held in refrigerator up to 2 days. Heat oven to 400 degrees. Brush 2 jelly-roll pans with remaining oil and divide vegetables between pans. Roast about 45 minutes, switching pans between oven racks about half way through cooking. When vegetables are browned and crisp, sprinkle with salt, pepper and parsley. Serves 10 to 12.

# Pistol Pete's No-Meat Chowder

*This vegetable stew can be beefed up by adding a pound of Sonoran beef jerky.*

| | |
|---|---|
| 1 | pound white beans (large or baby limas, small whites or great northerns) |
| 8 | cups water |
| 1-1/2 | teaspoons salt |
| 1 | cup onion, chopped |
| 1-1/2 | cups celery, chopped |
| 1/4 | cup butter or margarine |
| 1/4 | cup flour |
| 1/8 | teaspoon pepper |
| 3 | cups milk |
| 1 | 16 ounce can tomatoes |
| 1 | 16 ounce can whole kernel corn |
| 1/4 | pound Monterey Jack cheese OR sharp Cheddar, grated |

Rinse, sort and soak beans overnight (or quick-soak by covering beans with water, bringing to a boil and letting stand for 1 hour). Drain. In large kettle, cook beans in water with salt until tender (about 1 hour for limas, 2 to 3 hours for others). Do not drain. Meanwhile, saute onion and celery in butter in a medium saucepan. Blend in flour and pepper. Stir in milk and bring mixture to a boil. Add this mixture to beans and their liquid, along with remaining ingredients. Stir together and heat through. Serves 8 to 10.

# Fatbelly's Dutch Oven Baked Potatoes

| | |
|---|---|
| 6 | potatoes |
| 3 | tablespoons bacon fat or oil |
| 1 | teaspoon whole allspice |
| 8-10 | whole cloves |

Boil potatoes in their skins for about 5 minutes. Drain. Heat bacon fat or oil in Dutch oven over medium heat. When oil is hot, toss in allspice and cloves and roll each potato in the oil until coated, then place the lid tightly over oven and cook over low heat about 1 hour. Serves 6.

# Old Chisholm Mexican Beans

*"Oh, it's bacon and beans most every day, I'd as soon be a-eatin' prairie hay."*

| | |
|---|---|
| 1 | pound pinto beans |
| 8 | cups water |
| 2 | onions, sliced |
| 2 | garlic cloves, minced |
| 2 | teaspoons salt |
| 1/2 | pound fresh pork, diced |
| 1/2 | pound beef stew meat |
| 1/2 | cup tomato sauce mixed with |
| | equal amount of water |
| 1-1/2 | tablespoons chili powder |
| 1/4 | teaspoon each: black pepper, |
| | oregano, Mexican sage, cumin seed |

Pick over beans, cover with water and soak overnight. The next day, drain the beans and place in a large heavy kettle with a lid. Add 8 cups fresh water, 1 sliced onion, 1 teaspoon salt and 1 minced garlic clove. Place the beans over a medium-high fire and bring to a steady simmer. While the beans are simmering, dice the pork and place it in a skillet with 1 tablespoon oil and brown lightly. Add beef, the other onion and garlic and cook slowly until onion is tender but not brown. Add the tomato sauce and water, the chili powder and other seasonings; cook 5 minutes. Turn this mixture into the kettle with the beans and cook slowly 2 to 3 hours. Add additional water during cooking as necessary to keep beans from getting dry. Adjust seasoning to taste. Serves 6 to 8.

# Black-Eyed Peas and Rice

*Every region has its own version of beans and rice. This recipe is typical of the South.*

| | |
|---|---|
| 1 | pound black-eyed peas, cooked |
| 1/2 | pound salt pork, rind removed, |
| | diced into 1/2 inch pieces |
| 2 | red or green bell peppers, seeded, |
| | cored and cut into 1/2 inch pieces |
| 1 | medium onion, peeled and chopped |
| 6 | cloves garlic, peeled and finely chopped |
| 1 | cup converted rice |
| 2 | cups chicken broth |
| 2 | tablespoons dried oregano |
| 1 | teaspoon ground allspice |
| | Salt and freshly ground |
| | black pepper to taste |

Soak and cook blackeyes by standard method. Drain. In a large heavy kettle, saute salt pork until fat is rendered. Do not let it brown. Add peppers, onion and garlic and cook 5 more minutes over low heat. Add rice, stir for a minute, then add remaining ingredients. Cook, covered, until liquid is absorbed, about 20 minutes. Serves 6 to 8.

# "Just Ned" Larson's Cowboy Cabbage

*"This here is Great Grandpa Leese's recipe from the days when he was a Sheriff in Oklahoma Territory. The boys still hanker for this rootin'-tootin' favorite on roundup when the weather gits cold."*

| | |
|---|---|
| 4 | tablespoons bacon drippings |
| 1 | onion, chopped |
| 1 | head of cabbage, chopped |
| 1 | teaspoon garlic powder |
| | Salt to taste |
| | Lots of black pepper, |
| | "the more the better" |

Heat bacon drippings in large skillet. Add onions; cook until translucent. Stir in chopped cabbage. Sprinkle with garlic powder, salt and lots of black pepper. Cook cabbage until limp. Stir in more pepper and serve. Serves 4.

# Chili Fandango

*Fandango is a lively Mexican-American dance in triple time.*

| | |
|---|---|
| 3 | green bell peppers |
| 1/2 | pound bacon, sliced & diced |
| 1 | large onion, minced |
| 1 | clove garlic, minced |
| 6 | large tomatoes, peeled and diced |
| 1/2 | teaspoon salt |

Roast bell peppers over hot fire until black. Scrape off black skins and cut each pepper into several pieces. Fry bacon, onion and garlic in large cast iron skillet until crisp and brown. Add peppers, tomatoes and salt. Cook slowly over medium heat, covered, for 40 minutes. Serves 8.

# Big Foot Wallace's Tomatoes and Peppers

*This side vittle adds color and flavor to barbecued meats.*

| | |
|---|---|
| 8 | bell peppers |
| 3 | tablespoons olive oil |
| 8 | tomatoes, chopped |
| | Salt and pepper to taste |

Wash peppers and soak in ice water 1 hour. Dice into 1 inch squares, discarding the seeds and coarse membrane. Saute in olive oil until soft and slightly browned. Pour off excess oil and add chopped tomatoes. Season with salt and pepper. Cook slowly over low heat for 30 minutes. Serve as a side dish to barbecued meats. Makes 4 to 6 servings.

*"Speakin' of cowpunchers," says Rawhide Rawlins, "Up to a few years ago, there's mighty little known about cows and cow people. It puts me in mind of the eastern girl that asks her mother: 'Ma,' says she, 'do cowboys eat grass?' 'No, dear,' says the old lady, 'they're part human,' an' I don't know but the old gal had 'em sized up right. If they are human, they're a separate species."*

*Trails Plowed Under by Charles M. Russell, 1927.*

# Trail Pot Greens and Likker

*Put your waddy to work pickin' greens. Some edible weeds are dandelion, mustard, sorrel, pigweed, poke, and turnip tops.*

| | |
|---|---|
| 2 | pounds greens |
| 1/4 | pound salt pork |
| | Water to cover |

Trim off roots and tough stems and discard imperfect leaves; wash thoroughly. Fry salt pork in Dutch oven over moderate heat. Place greens into pot and cover with water. Simmer until tender. Serve with biscuits or corn bread. Serves 6.

# Corn Chowder

| | |
|---|---|
| 1 | cup potatoes, diced |
| 1 | cup boiling water |
| 3 | slices bacon, cut small |
| 1 | medium onion, chopped |
| 1-1/2 | cups corn, fresh or canned |
| 1 | cup milk |
| | Parsley for garnish |

Cook potatoes in boiling water 10 to 15 minutes. Fry bacon until some of the fat cooks out. Add onion; cook until onion is soft and bacon is browned. Add to potatoes then add corn. Add milk, salt and pepper to taste. Cook 10 minutes. Sprinkle on parsley before serving. If you prefer a thickened chowder, blend 1 tablespoon flour with some of the liquid before adding milk. Serves 4 to 6.

A cowpuncher got lucky in a card game in Cheyenne and took his big bank roll to Chicago. "The minute I hit the burg," he says, "I shed my cow garments an' get into white man's harness...all the gearin' known to civilized man. When I put on all this rig, I sure look human; that is, I think so. But them shorthorns know me, an' by the way they trim that roll, it looks like somebody's pinned a card on my back with the word 'EASY' in big letters....

15 drinks) "I was sizing me up while roll) but I'm too late. 'Neighbor, you're a

I ain't been there a week before"...(after more than unconscious and later come to and this feller was I'm dressin. I go through myself (for the bank Somebody beat me to it. This stranger speaks: long way from your range'.

"You call the turn," didn't see a burn watching you get and punchers dress

says I, "but how did you read my iron?" "I on you," he says, "it's your ways, while I'm into your garments. Now, humans dress up down. When you raised, the first thing you put on is your hat...."

Trails Plowed Under by
Charles M. Russell, 1927.

# DAY'S END

## Main Vittles

# Hot-n-jumpin' Sourdough Chicken Fried Steaks

*This recipe from Manflo Ranch is one of Bryan "Manflo" Jones' prize winning favorites of his Cowboy Cookin' Catering Company.*

| | |
|---|---|
| 4 | pounds tri-tip steaks, cut into squares about 4 inches x 1 inch thick |
| 2 | fresh jalapeno chilies stemmed, seeded & minced |
| 1 | cup sourdough starter (page 2) |
| 1 | cup flour, seasoned with black pepper, crushed red pepper, salt, sage and thyme |
| | Olive oil |

Using a sharp knife, cut a small pocket into center of steaks and fill with minced jalapeno chiles. Brush steaks with olive oil and grill 4 to 5 inches from medium coals, turning once, until meat reaches desired doneness, about 7 minutes each side for medium. Remove steaks and dip in sour dough starter. Heat oil in skillet; combine seasonings with flour; dredge each steak in flour mixture and fry in hot oil until brown on both sides, turning once. Serves 6 to 8.

# Chicken & Dumplings

| | |
|---|---|
| 1 | 3 to 4 pound stewing chicken, cut up |
| 4 | celery stalk tops, chopped |
| 1 | medium carrot, thinly sliced |
| 2 | sprigs parsley, minced |
| 1 | teaspoon salt |
| 1/8 | teaspoon pepper |
| 5 | cups water |
| 1/2 | cup flour |
| | Dumplings (recipe below) |

Remove excess fat from chicken. Place chicken, giblets (except liver), neck, celery, carrot, onion, parsley, salt, pepper and water in Dutch oven. Cover and heat to boiling; reduce heat to low. Cook over low heat about 2 hours or until juice of chicken is no longer pink when centers of thickest pieces are cut. Remove chicken and vegetables from Dutch oven. Skim

1/2 cup fat from broth and reserve. Remove remaining broth; reserve 4 cups. Remove chicken from the bones.

Heat reserved fat in Dutch oven over low heat. Stir in 1/2 cup flour. Cook, stirring constantly, until mixture is smooth and bubbly; remove from heat. Season with salt and pepper. Stir in remaining broth. Heat to boiling, stirring constantly. Boil and stir 1 minute. Return chicken and vegetables to Dutch oven; heat until hot. Make dumplings and drop dough by spoonfuls onto hot chicken mixture. (Do not sink dough into liquid). Cook uncovered over low heat 10 minutes. Cover and cook 10 minutes longer. Serves 4 to 6.

# Dumplings:

| | |
|---|---|
| 1-1/2 | cups flour |
| 1/2 | teaspoon salt |
| 3 | teaspoons baking powder |
| 1 | egg |
| 2 to 3 | tablespoons milk |

Mix dry ingredients together and make a well in the center of the flour. Drop egg into well and beat with a fork. Add milk slowly until all flour is worked into dough and makes a ball. Cover and let dough rest in the refrigerator for 30 minutes before dropping it by spoonfuls onto the hot chicken mixture. Cook for 10 minutes uncovered over low heat, then cover and cook 10 minutes longer.

# The Roundup

Ranchers in Texas began raising cattle as early as 1830. Adopting the methods of the vaqueros of Northern Mexico, ranchers allowed their cattle to graze over public lands, and the era of the open range began. When the cattle strayed too far, the rancher hired hands to help in a cow hunt to bring the cattle home. Twice annually, cowboys herded the cattle to a central place, where they sorted them according to their markings; and marked the new calves with the owner's brand. They separated diseased or injured animals from the herd and counted and selected cattle to go to market. Roundups required more skill than any other phase of a cowboy's job. Like an athletic contest, much friendly rivalry developed, and when the work was finished, the cowboys often held a large celebration called a rodeo, which attracted as many as several hundred cowboys. They competed in bareback riding, steer wrestling, calf roping and other tests of skill.

## Sonoran Beef Jerky

Jerky was a staple for cowboys as it was a way to preserve meat in batches light and small enough to carry on the trail.

| | |
|---|---|
| 3 | pounds lean beef, thinly sliced, 1/4 inch or less |
| 1/2 | cup water |
| 1/2 | cup lime juice |
| 9 | garlic cloves |

Combine water and lime juice. Press garlic into liquid; or puree mixture in blender. Place beef slices into a shallow bowl and cover with the garlic mixture, turning beef to coat all pieces. Marinate overnight. Traditionally, jerky was hung on a line, or spread on a rack and air dried for 12 hours or more, up to a week, until fully dehydrated. For oven drying, place jerky on a baking sheet or oven rack at 250 degrees for 5 hours or until dry. Store in closed containers in a cool dry place. Makes about 12 ounces jerky.

## Rozzi Warren's Tamale Pie

Rozzi of Cowboy Cookin' contributed this popular recipe.

| | |
|---|---|
| 1 | pound ground beef |
| 1 | onion, chopped |
| 1 | cup cream style corn |
| 2 | cups pitted ripe olives |
| 1 | 8 ounce can tomato sauce |
| 1 | egg |
| 16 | ounces canned milk |
| 1 | tablespoon chili powder |
| 1 | tablespoon garlic powder |
| | Salt and pepper to taste |
| 1/3 | cup corn meal |

Brown ground beef and onions in a 10 inch Dutch oven. Combine creamed corn, olives, tomato sauce and egg with milk. Add to beef mixture. Bring to a boil. Add seasonings and adjust to taste. Reduce heat. Add corn meal and simmer until mixture thickens. Cover and place in oven at 350 degrees for 30 minutes, or until set. Serves 6.

# Mexican Grilled Steak

| | |
|---|---|
| 2 | 1 to 1-1/2 pound beef flank steaks |
| 2 | limes, juiced (about 1/2 cup) |
| 4 | cloves garlic, crushed |
| 1/3 | cup fresh oregano leaves, chopped; or 2 tablespoons dried oregano, crushed |
| 2 | tablespoons olive oil |
| 2 | teaspoons salt |
| 1/2 | teaspoon pepper |

Place beef steaks in a shallow glass or plastic dish. Mix remaining ingredients; pour over beef. Cover and refrigerate at least 8 hours but no longer than 24 hours, turning beef occasionally. Cover and grill beef 4 to 5 inches from medium coals, turning once, until meat reaches desired doneness, about 7 minutes each side for medium. Cut beef across grain at slanted angle into thin slices. Serve with tortillas and guacamole if desired. Serves 8.

*Cattlemen made large profits in the thirty years after the Civil War. A steer that cost $5 in Texas or Wyoming would be worth $40 or $50 in Chicago. The cattle industry boomed and some ranchers made hugh fortunes.*

# Cattlemen's Club Roast Prime Ribs of Beef & yorkshire pudding

| | |
|---|---|
| 1 | 4 to 6 pound standing rib roast |
| | Salt and pepper |

Allow 3/4 pound per person. Rub salt and pepper over roast. Stand the roast in a shallow baking pan or place fat side up on a rack. Insert meat thermometer in center of the thickest part of the meat so that it does not touch a bone or rest in fat. Do not add water; do not cover pan. Roast in oven at 325 degrees to desired doneness. See timetable below. Allow roast to set 15 to 20 minutes before carving. Since the meat continues to cook after removal from oven, the roast should be removed when the thermometer registers 5 to 10 degrees below the desired doneness. Serves 6 to 8.

*Timetable for roasting: 18 to 20 minutes per pound for rare; 140 degrees on thermometer; 22 to 25 minutes per pound for medium; 160 degrees on thermometer; 27 to 30 minutes per pound for well done; 170 degrees on thermometer.*

# Yorkshire Pudding

| | |
|---|---|
| 1-1/2 | cups all-purpose flour |
| 3/4 | teaspoon salt |
| 1-1/2 | cups milk |
| 3 | eggs |
| 3/4 | cup pan drippings |

About 40 minutes before serving time, combine all ingredients and stir well just until smooth. Preheat a 13"x9"x2" baking dish or 8 muffin cups. Remove roast from oven. Increase oven temperature to 400 degrees. Measure pan drippings, and add melted shortening, if necessary, to reach 3/4 cup. Place hot drippings into baking dish, or distribute equally in muffin cups; pour in batter. Bake about 30 minutes until pudding rises on the sides and turns golden brown. Cut into squares and serve immediately with roast.

# Cast Iron Cooking

Cooking on the Open Trail

For centuries, heavy cast iron cookware has survived from generation to generation, from the open hearth to the open trail. One of the most versatile of these cookwares is the Dutch oven, a heavy pot, usually 10 to 20 inches in diameter, with a tight fitting lid. The pots designed for outdoor cooking often have short legs and a rimmed lid, so that coals may be placed under the pot and on top of the lid. Heat from the bottom and the top of the pot create a cooking condition similar to a conventional oven in which food may be baked, braised or roasted. A Dutch oven was an important utensil for chuck wagon cooks, who used them for everything from bacon to beans, from stews to cobblers. Any recipe that can be cooked in a skillet on top of the stove, or in a roasting pot or baking dish in the oven, may be cooked in the Dutch oven outdoors.

# Number of Charcoals Needed For Dutch Oven Cooking

Most Dutch ovens are 10" to 16" in diameter. Follow this formula for the number of coals and place 1/3 of coals under the Dutch oven and 2/3 of the coals on the lid.

FOR MODERATE HEAT: The diameter of the Dutch oven multiplied by 2 equals the number of coals to use; i.e. 12" pot x 2 = 24 coals; 1/3 or 8 under the pot and 2/3 or 16 on lid.

FOR HIGH HEAT: The diameter of the Dutch oven multiplied by 3.

TO MAINTAIN HEAT OVER AN HOUR, IGNITE 10 TO 12 EXTRA COALS AND ADD 4 OR 5 COALS AFTER EACH 20 TO 30 MINUTES OF COOKING.

"Everybody knows that Pecos Bill
Southwest, invented most of the things conne
was a great roper. In fact, he invented ropin
said that his rope was as long as t
conservative say that it was at least
used to rope a herd of cattle at one

ythical cowboy hero of the

with the cow business. He

Old timers who knowed him

quator, although the more

feet shorter on one end. He

w."

"One time, Pecos Bill's hoss broke a leg, leaving Bill afoot with about a hundred miles to go that afternoon. He slung his saddle over his shoulder and set off a-hikin' and a'swearin. Soon, he come to a 10 foot rattlesnake and just to be fair, Bill give the snake the first three bites. Wasn't long the old rattler yelled for mercy and Bill picked up the snake and the saddle and started on, waving that snake at the gila monsters. About 50 miles further on, a big old mountain lion jumped off a cliff and landed on Bill's neck. Bill laid down the saddle and the snake and went into action. In about 3 minutes, the old lion give up and Bill cinched the saddle on him and rode off whoppin' and yellin' and quirtin' him down the flank with the rattlesnake.

Directly, he saw a chuck wagon with a bunch of cowboys squattin' around it. He rode up to that wagon, splittin' the air with his war whoops, with that old lion a'screechin' and that snake singin' his rattles. When he come to the fire, he grabbed the old cougar by the ear, jerked him back on his haunches, stepped off him, hung his snake around his neck and looked the outfit over. Them cowboys sat there sayin' less than nothing.

Bill was hungry and seein' a boilerful of beans cookin' on the fire, he scooped up a few handfuls and swallowed them, washin' them down with a few gallons of boilin' coffee out of the pot. Wipin' his mouth on a prickly pear catcus, Bill asked: 'Who the hell is boss around here?'

A big feller, about 8 feet tall, with 7 pistols and 9 bowie knives in his belt, rose up and takin' off his hat, said: 'Stranger, I was; but you be'."

*Branding Irons*

# Son-of-a-Bitch Stew

This concoction calls for using the liver, heart, brains, sweetbreads, kidneys and marrow-gut of a freshly killed young steer. The marrow-gut, about 3 feet, is the tube connecting the two stomachs of cud-chewing animals. It is especially good while the calf is still nursing because it is tender, nourishing and resembles marrow. There are many variations of this stew although generally the preparation called for cutting the entrails into small cubes, frying them in beef suet, then covering with water, salt and pepper and cooking for 2 to 3 hours.

# Abilene Alan's Kick-Ass Chili

*This award winning chili is reminiscent of chuck wagon chile-flavored stews of the cattle drives. Tenderfoots should add the hot chiles one at a time and adjust to taste.*

| | |
|---|---|
| 3 | tablespoons bacon drippings or cooking oil |
| 2 | large red onions, coarsely chopped |
| 4 | pounds beef chuck or round steak, coarsely ground |
| 3 | garlic cloves, minced |
| 3 | dried red chilies, roasted 1 minute over high heat & minced |
| 2 | tablespoons ground cumin |
| 2 | tablespoons brown sugar |
| 2 | teaspoons dried oregano leaves |
| 1 | 16 ounce can tomato sauce |
| 1-3/4 | cup water |
| 1-1/2 | tablespoons salt |
| 1 | cup corn flour (masa harina) |
| 1 | 16 ounce can kidney beans (optional) |

Heat oil in a heavy Dutch oven over medium heat. Add onions and cook until they are translucent. Combine the beef with the garlic, minced chile, cumin, brown sugar and oregano. Add meat and spice mixtures to the pot with the onions. Break up any lumps with a fork and continue to cook. Add tomato sauce, water and salt. Bring to a boil, lower heat and simmer, uncovered, for 1 hour. Stir in the corn flour to achieve desired consistency. Cook 15 minutes longer, stirring. Adjust seasonings to taste. Serves 8.

# Dodge City Beef Pot Roast

| | |
|---|---|
| 4-5 | pounds lean boneless chuck roast OR 7 - bone roast |
| 1 | quart water |
| 1 | tablespoon sugar |
| 1 | stalk celery, sliced |
| 2 | onions, sliced |
| 1 | tablespoon salt |
| 1 | teaspoon pepper |
| 1/2 | teaspoon curry powder |
| 1/2 | teaspoon cinnamon |
| 1/2 | teaspoon allspice |
| 1 | teaspoon dry mustard |
| 1-1/2 | carrots (per person) |
| 2 | medium potatoes (per person) |

Combine water, sugar, celery, onions, salt, pepper and spices. Pour mixture over meat and allow to stand overnight in refrigerator. Remove the meat and cook in a 300 degree oven for 3 to 4 hours. During the last hour, add the carrots and potatoes, placing carrots on top of meat. Thicken the drippings if desired and serve with the roast and vegetables. Serves 6-8.

# Smoked Buffalo or Venison Jerky (Dry Preparation)

| 5 | pounds venison or buffalo roast, sliced with the grain in thin 1/8 inch strips |
| 1/2 | cup salt |
| 1/4 | cup sugar |
| 3 | tablespoons black pepper |
| 2 | teaspoons garlic powder |

For easy slicing, chill meat and slice with the grain 1/8 inch thick, about 1/2 inch wide and 2 to 3 inches long. Remove any major tendons and tenderize, if necessary, by grasping each piece with hands and jerking lengthwise. Sprinkle both sides of meat strips with seasonings and lay pieces in a single layer in a container and allow to stand in a cool place for 24 hours or more to absorb seasonings. When ready to cook, place meat slices in a single layer on racks in a smoker oven over green alder, hickory or mesquite wood chips. Smoke over low heat 5 to 6 hours or until dry but not hard and brittle. Cool. Store in closed containers in a cool dry place. Makes about 1-1/2 pounds jerky.

# Trail Hand's Catch of the Day

Make that waddy work and catch somethin'! Butcher of Cowboy Cookin' sez "this here is some of the best fixin's around but watch out for the bones."

| 10 | potatoes, sliced |
| 4 | onions, sliced |
| 2 | dried red chiles, chopped |
| 4 | tablespoons cooking oil |
| 3 | pounds trout, or as many as caught |
| | Cornmeal (2 heapin' handfuls) |
| | Salt and pepper |

Heat 2 tablespoons cooking oil or a small chunk of lard in a large Dutch oven. Add sliced potatoes and onions in layers, sprinkling each layer with salt, pepper and chopped chiles. Cover and put in the fire, with coals over and under the pot, for 20 to 30 minutes, or until potatoes are almost cooked. If using an indoor oven, bake at 350 degrees for about 1 hour.

Clean trout. Heat remaining oil in skillet. Roll fish in cornmeal, salt and pepper. Fry in hot oil about 5 minutes per side. Lay trout over top of potatoes in Dutch oven and cook for 10 more minutes. Serves 8 to 10.

## Cattle Drive Formation

*The usual trail drive formation was made up of 11 types of riders, with 1 man for every 150 head of cattle. Cattle were rounded up, branded and driven by the hundred of thousands north to a rail head from which they could be shipped in open cars to Kansas City and on to the stock yards of Chicago. Cowboys were hired on at $25 to $40 per month to make the long drive which might take several months. Good trail bosses, who could handle the dangers encountered along the route and maintain discipline among the cowboys earned as much as $125 per month.*

*Herding Cattle*

## "Grab a Plate & Growl" Beef or Lamb Stew

| 1-1/2 | pounds beef OR lamb stew meat, cut into 2" cubes |
|---|---|
| 3 | tablespoons flour |
| 1-1/2 | teaspoons salt |
| 1/4 | teaspoons pepper |
| 2 | tablespoons vegetable oil |
| 2 | cups water |
| 1/2 | cup onion, chopped |
| 1-2 | cloves garlic, minced |
| 1 | cup celery, cut in 2" pieces |
| 4 | large carrots, cut in 2" pieces |
| 1 | cup frozen peas or green beans |
| 1 | tablespoon catsup |
| 1 | tablespoon Worcestershire sauce |
| 1 | tablespoon parsley, chopped |

Combine flour, salt and pepper in a paper bag. Shake meat cubes in seasoned flour until well coated. Heat oil in skillet to medium high and brown meat well on all sides, turning occasionally. When browned, stir in any remaining flour mixture and add water, onion, garlic and celery. Bring to a boil, then cover and simmer for 1 hour or more, until meat is almost tender. A half hour before serving, add carrots and peas. Bring to a boil again, reduce heat and stir in catsup,

Worcestershire and parsley. Simmer, covered, for one half hour. Lift meat and vegetables onto serving platter and thicken pan broth with flour and water if desired. Serves 4-6.

## Dutch Oven Roasted Quail, Pheasant, Prairie Grouse or Rabbit

Game birds were always plentiful on the American prairie, but pheasant, which was to become one of the most popular, was introduced to North America from China and first seen on the frontier in the 1880's. Rabbits were abundant on the prairies.

| 1/4 | cup flour |
|---|---|
| 1 | teaspoon salt |
| 1/2 | teaspoon pepper |
| 2 | onions, sliced |
| 2 | tablespoons bacon fat or cooking oil |
| 2 | 2 to 3 pound pheasants OR grouse, cleaned, cut up, semi-boneless and ready to cook OR |
| 2 | 2 pound rabbits, cut up |
| 1-1/2 | cups water |
| 1 | cup milk |
| 3 | tablespoons flour |
| 1 | teaspoon salt |
| | Dash of pepper and paprika |

Combine flour, salt and pepper in a bag and add bird or rabbit pieces a few at a time; shake to coat. In a deep cast iron skillet with a lid, brown pieces slowly in hot oil. Arrange onions on top of meat, add 1 cup of water, cover tightly and cook over low heat until tender, about 1 hour. Remove meat; measure liquid in pan and add water, if necessary to equal 1 cup. Combine milk, flour, salt and pepper and stir into pan liquid. Cook, stirring constantly, until thickened. Before serving, sprinkle meat pieces with paprika and serve gravy separately. Serves 4 to 6.

# Tex-Mex Pork Roast

| 1 | 4 to 5 pound boneless double pork loin roast, rolled and tied |
|---|---|
| 1/2 | teaspoon salt |
| 1/2 | teaspoon garlic salt |
| 1/2 | teaspoon chili powder |
| 1 | cup apple jelly |
| 1 | cup catsup |
| 2 | tablespoons vinegar |
| 1 | teaspoon chili powder |
| 1/2 | cup corn chips, crushed |

Rub roast on all sides with salt, garlic salt and 1/2 teaspoon chili powder. Place roast, fat side up, in a shallow roasting pan. Insert meat thermometer into thickest part of roast, making sure thermometer does not touch fat. Bake at 325 degrees for about 2 hours or until thermometer registers 165 degrees. Combine jelly, catsup, vinegar and 1 teaspoon chili powder in a small saucepan. Bring to a boil; reduce heat and simmer, uncovered, 2 minutes. Brush roast with jelly mixture. Sprinkle with corn chips. Return to oven. Bake at 325 degrees for 10 to 15 minutes or until thermometer registers 170 degrees. Serve with sauce. Serves 12.

## Trail Rider Positions

| Trail boss | Rides ahead of the herd to scout for a campsite near water and pasture to bed the cattle down for the night. |
|---|---|
| Point riders | The most experienced riders leading the herd in the desired direction. |
| Flank riders & Swing riders | Ride alongside the herd to keep cattle from straying & fetching those that do. |
| Drag riders | Ride in the rear of herd to push and prod the slow cattle along the trail. |
| Wrangler | Drives and cares for the remuda, 100 or more saddle horses, and fetches water, collects wood or cow chips & assists the cook. |
| Chuck wagon | Cook drives wagon ahead of herd from one campsite to the next. |

# 2-Gun Elmer's Barbecued Ribs

| 4 | 1/2 pound racks of fresh pork loin back ribs |
| 3 | cups water |
| 1/2 | cup soy sauce |
| 2 | tablespoons cornstarch |

Place pork back ribs in Dutch oven; add water. Heat to boiling; reduce heat. Cover and simmer 5 minutes. Remove ribs; drain. Return to Dutch oven. Mix soy sauce and corn starch; brush on ribs. Continue brushing both sides of ribs with soy sauce mixture every 10 minutes, until mixture is gone, about 30 minutes. Grill ribs about 6" from medium coals, brushing with barbecue sauce every 3 minutes, until ribs are done and meat begins to pull away from the bone, about 20 minutes. Cut into serving pieces. Serve with remaining sauce. Serves 4.

# Jed's Barbecued Beef Brisket

| 1 | 4 to 5 pound boneless beef brisket |
| 1 | medium onion, quartered |
| 1 | garlic clove, crushed |
| 1 | bay leaf |
| 2 | cups catsup |
| 1 | cup water |
| 1/4 | cup lemon juice |
| 1/4 | cup Worcestershire sauce |
| 2 | tablespoons sugar |
| 1 | tablespoon salt |
| 2 | tablespoons liquid smoke |
| 2 | teaspoons celery seed |
| 1 | teaspoon chili powder |

# Barbecue Sauce

| 1 | cup water |
| 1 | cup catsup |
| 1/4 | cup packed brown sugar |
| 1/4 | cup vinegar |
| 1/4 | cup Worcestershire sauce |
| 1 | tablespoon celery seed |
| 1 | teaspoon chili powder |
| 1 | teaspoon salt |
| | Few drops of red pepper sauce |
| | Dash of pepper |

Heat all ingredients to boiling. Simmer 10 minutes. This sauce may be used on pork, chicken or beef. Yields 2-1/2 cups

About 4 hours before serving: Place brisket, onion, garlic and bay leaf in a covered kettle with just enough water to cover and bring to a boil. Reduce heat and simmer 2-1/2 hours until tender. Preheat oven to 325 degrees. In medium saucepan over medium heat, combine catsup, 1 cup water and remaining ingredients; heat to boiling. Drain meat; place in foil lined shallow baking pan. Brush meat with catsup mixture; bake 45 minutes, basting occasionally. Over medium heat, heat remaining catsup mixture; serve with meat. Makes 10 to 12 servings.

Vital Vittles

# Breads & Sweets

## Cornbread

| | |
|---|---|
| 1-1/2 | cups yellow cornmeal |
| 1 | cup all-purpose flour, sifted |
| 1 | tablespoon baking powder |
| 1-1/4 | teaspoons salt |
| 3/4 | cup unsalted butter, melted and cooled |
| 2 | large eggs, lightly beaten |
| 1-1/2 | cups milk |

Preheat oven to 375 degrees. Butter a 9 inch square pan. In a mixing bowl, sift together the cornmeal, flour, baking powder and salt. Add the butter, eggs and milk and stir until just combined. Pour into pan and bake about 40 minutes; or divide mix into corn stick mold pan and bake 20 minutes. Or double the recipe, pour into a greased heavy cast iron skillet that has been preheated. Bake for 25 to 30 minutes. Yields 6-9 servings.

## Wichita's Whole Wheat Bread

| | |
|---|---|
| 4 | cups wheat flour |
| 2 | cups white flour |
| 2 | teaspoons salt |
| 2-1/2 | cups warm water (110 degrees) |
| 2 | packages active dry yeast |
| 1/4 | cup soft shortening |
| 1/4 | cup honey or brown sugar |

Mix flours and salt together in large bowl. Dissolve yeast in water. Add the yeast mixture to the flours reserving 3 cups of flour for later addition. Mix well. Stir in remaining flour. Knead well, adding flour to keep dough from sticking. Place dough in greased large bowl. Cover and let rise until doubled. Punch down dough. Divide into 2 parts and form 2 loaves. Place into loaf pans and let rise again until doubled. Bake in preheated 375 degree oven about 45 minutes. Lower heat a bit if loaves are getting too brown.

# Packsaddle Pete's Favorite Sourdough French Bread

| | |
|---|---|
| 1/2 | cup milk |
| 1 | cup water |
| 1-1/2 | teaspoons vegetable oil |
| 1 | package active dry yeast |
| 1/4 | cup warm water (about 110 degrees) |
| 1-1/2 | tablespoons sugar |
| 2-1/2 | teaspoons salt |
| 4-3/4 | cups all-purpose flour |
| 3/4 | cup sour dough starter |
| 1 | egg white mixed with |
| | 1 tablespoon cold water |

Mix water, milk and vegetable oil. Bring to a boil and then cool. Dissolve yeast in warm water. Add yeast, sugar and salt to cooled milk mixture and stir until sugar and salt are dissolved. Add flour and sour dough starter. Stir well, but do not knead. Place in a large bowl, cover and let rise until double in bulk, about 1-1/2 hours.

Turn onto a lightly floured board and divide into two portions. Pat or roll each portion into a 15"x10" rectangle. Beginning at the long end, roll up tightly and seal edge by pinching together. With a hand on each end, roll gently back and forth to taper ends. Place on baking sheet. With a sharp knife, make 1/8" deep cuts diagonally along loaf about 2" apart. Cover and let rise until a little more than double. Preheat oven to 425 degrees. Bake 15 minutes. Reduce heat to 350 degrees and bake 15 to 20 minutes longer. Brush top and sides with a mixture of 1 egg white and 1 tablespoon cold water. Bake 5 minutes longer. Cool. Makes 2 loaves.

# Spoon Bread

| | |
|---|---|
| 2-1/2 | cups milk |
| 2 | teaspoons sugar |
| 1 | teaspoon salt |
| 1 | cup yellow corn meal |
| 3 | eggs, separated |
| 3 | tablespoons butter |

Place milk in top of double boiler and heat to boiling point. Add salt, sugar and corn meal, stirring constantly to prevent lumps. Cook 4 minutes and pour slowly over beaten yolks. Add butter and beat until it is melted. Fold in stiffly beaten whites and pour in greased deep casserole or souffle dish. Bake at 400 degrees for 45 minutes. Serves 8.

# Cowboy Terms

| | |
|---|---|
| Bronco | A wild horse |
| Maverick | An unbranded animal |
| Dogie | An undersized calf |
| Muley | A hornless cow |
| Paint | A horse with irregular patches of white |
| Remuda | A range outfit's collection of saddle horses |
| String | A cowboy's mount or line of horses |
| Chuck | Food |
| Cookie | A ranch/chuck wagon cook |
| Nighthawk | A cowboy who guards the herds at night and sleeps during the day |
| Nester | A squatter on government land, usually to farm |
| Tenderfoot | A person new to the job |
| Waddie | Temporary hand hired when a ranch is short of help |
| Road Agent | Cowboy slang for robber |
| Rustler | Cattle thief |
| Cow town | Town at the end of the trail where cowboys delivered their herds |
| Boot Hill | Cow town cemeteries |

# Navajo Fry Bread

| 4 | cups all-purpose flour |
|---|---|
| 1 | tablespoon baking powder |
| 1 | teaspoon salt |
| 2 | tablespoons nonfat dry milk powder |
| 1-1/2 | cups warm water |
| 1-2 | cups solid shortening or lard, for frying |

Combine flour, baking powder, salt and dry milk powder in a large mixing bowl. Gradually stir in warm water. Mix until dough forms a ball and comes clean from edge of bowl. You may need to add a little additional water. Knead dough with your hands until well mixed and dough is elastic. Divide dough into 6 large pieces and roll into balls. Using palms of your hands, pat out dough into circles that are about 1/2 inch thick.

Melt shortening in a large skillet. You will need about 3/4 inch of melted fat. Heat to 400 degrees. Slip a rounded, flat piece of dough into the hot fat - it will start to rise to the top. When the underside is brown, turn over and brown the other side. Drain on paper towels. Repeat with remaining dough. (For a snack, divide dough into small portions to make 2 inch balls. After cooking and draining, sprinkle with confectioners sugar or drizzle with honey.) Yields 6 large portions or 8 to 10 snack portions.

# Cowboy's Crunchy Sourdough Cornmeal Bread

| 1 | package active dry yeast |
|---|---|
| 2 | cups warm water (about 110 degrees) |
| 3/4 | cup sourdough starter |
| 1/3 | cup vegetable shortening, melted |
| 2 | cups yellow cornmeal |
| 6 | cups all-purpose flour |
| 2 | teaspoons salt |

Soften yeast in water for several minutes. Stir in starter, oil and cornmeal. With a heavy spoon, gradually stir in enough flour to make a stiff dough. Turn dough out onto a board and knead about 5 minutes until smooth, adding flour as necessary to prevent sticking. Place dough in a greased bowl, grease top, cover and let rise in a warm place until double in bulk, about 1-1/2 hours. Punch dough down and divide in half. Knead gently until smooth. Shape each piece into a round. Smooth top and pull down slightly to make a seam underneath. Place loaves on a baking sheet, cover and let rise until double, about 1-1/2 hours. Bake at 375 degrees abut 30 minutes, or until top is golden brown. Cool on racks. Makes 2 loaves.

# Kaycee Peach Pie

|       | Pastry for two crust pie |
| ----- | ------------------------ |
| 1/3   | cup sugar |
| 1/3   | cup all-purpose flour |
| 1/4   | teaspoon ground nutmeg |
| 6     | cups (about 6 to 8 medium) peaches, uniformly sliced |
| 1     | teaspoon lemon juice |
| 1     | tablespoon margarine or butter |

Heat oven to 400 degrees. Prepare pastry. Mix sugar, flour and cinnamon in large bowl. Stir in peaches and lemon juice. Turn into pastry-lined pie plate. Dot with margarine. Cover with top pastry and cut slits in it; seal and flute edges. Cover edge with a 2 to 3 inch strip of aluminum foil to prevent excessive browning. Remove foil during last 15 minutes of baking. Bake about 45 minutes or until crust is brown and juice begins to bubble through slits in crust. Cool in pie plate on wire rack. Serve warm or cool. Yields 8 servings.

# Indian Pudding

|       | |
| ----- | ------------------------ |
| 1/2   | cup yellow cornmeal |
| 4     | cups milk; scalded |
| 2     | tablespoons butter, melted |
| 1/2   | cup molasses |
| 1     | teaspoon cinnamon |
| 1/2   | teaspoon ground ginger |
| 1     | teaspoon salt |
| 2     | eggs, separated |
|       | Whipped unsweetened heavy cream |

Heat milk just until it boils. Place the cornmeal in the top of a double boiler, over boiling water, and gradually add the scalded milk. Stir constantly and continue to cook for 20 minutes. Remove from heat and stir in the butter, molasses, spices, salt, and egg yolks. Set aside to cool slightly. In a clean bowl, beat the egg whites until stiff but not dry. Fold into the pudding mixture. Turn the batter into a greased baking dish and bake for approximately 40 minutes in preheated 350 degree oven. Let cool and serve with whipped cream. Serves 6 - 8.

# Mis' Mattie's Fruit Cobbler

*From Mis' Mattie's kitchen in Russellville, Alabama, to the trails of Texas, taken there by her boy who run off to Waco to work stock.*

| | |
|---|---|
| 3 | cups fruit, cleaned and sliced as for pie |
| 3 | tablespoons butter |
| 1 | cup sugar |
| 1/2 | teaspoon cinnamon |
| 3 | tablespoons flour |
| 1 | cup flour |
| 1-1/2 | teaspoons baking powder |
| 2 | tablespoons sugar |
| 1/2 | teaspoon salt |
| 1/3 | cup vegetable oil |
| 1 | egg, slightly beaten |
| 3 | tablespoons milk |

Prepare fruit and arrange it on the bottom of a greased 8"x8" baking dish or a 10" Dutch oven. Cut butter into sugar, cinnamon and 2 tablespoons flour until it resembles fine crumbs. Sprinkle over fruit. Combine remaining dry ingredients. Make a well in the flour mixture and stir in oil, milk and egg. Blend with a fork until moistened. Spoon by tablespoonfuls over top of fruit. Bake at 350 degrees for 25 to 30 minutes. Serves 6 to 8.

# Calico Queen's Gingerbread

| | |
|---|---|
| 1/3 | cup shortening |
| 1 | cup sugar |
| 2 | eggs |
| 1/2 | cup molasses |
| 1 | cup sour cream |
| 2 | cups sifted flour |
| 1 | teaspoon baking soda |
| 1/2 | teaspoon salt |
| 1-1/2 | teaspoons ground ginger |
| 1/4 | teaspoon ground cloves |

Cream shortening and sugar; add eggs, one at a time, beating well after each addition. Stir in molasses and sour cream. Blend in the dry ingredients, and beat 2 minutes. Bake in greased 9 x 13 inch pan in a preheated 350 degree oven until cake tests done. Yields 12 servings.

# Apple Crisp

| | |
|---|---|
| 8-9 | tart apples, like Granny Smith |
| 1-1/2 | cups quick oats |
| 1-1/2 | cups brown sugar |
| 1 | cup flour |
| 2 | teaspoons cinnamon |
| 1/4 | teaspoon nutmeg |
| 3/4 | cup buttter |

Arrange apple slices in a buttered deep baking dish. If apples are tart, add a sprinkling of granulated sugar over slices. Combine oats, sugar, flour and spices. Cut in butter. Mix well and spread over apples. Bake at 350 degrees for 35 to 40 minutes. Serve warm with cheese wedges or whipped cream. Serves 6 to 8.

# Rice Pudding

| 3 | cups milk |
| 1/2 | cup granulated sugar |
| 2 | cups cooked rice |
| 1 | cup raisins |
| 2-3 | tablespoons butter |
| 1 | teaspoon vanilla extract |

Combine milk, sugar, rice, raisins and butter in saucepan. Simmer 20 to 30 minutes, or until thick. Remove from heat and stir in vanilla. Serves 4 to 6.

# Everything But the Dishwater Squaw Cake

A moist cake made without eggs or butter, ingredients often hard to find on the trail. Traditionally, trail cooks used mild flavored beef or pork lard, rendered from the kidney fat. Throw in just about everything but the dishwater.

| 1 | cup raisins OR any dried fruit |
| 2 | cups water |
| 4 | cups flour |
| 1 | teaspoon baking powder |
| 1 | teaspoon baking soda |
| 1/2 | teaspoon salt |
| 1 | cup granulated sugar |
| 1/2 | cup dark brown sugar OR 1/3 cup molasses |
| 1 | teaspoon each: ground allspice, ground cinnamon, ground cloves and ground nutmeg |
| 1 | cup melted shortening |

Place raisins or other dired fruit in saucepan and cover with water. Bring to a boil and simmer for 15 minutes. Combine all dry ingredients and molasses, if using. Stir in melted shortening until batter forms a smooth paste. Add raisins and the remaining liquid to the batter. Pour into a greased 9 inch cake pan and bake about 1-1/2 hours at 325 degrees. Allow to cool and place in a tin overnight before serving. This moist cake was a popular dessert on the trail, and was also used as a breakfast bread. Serves 8 to 10.

# Mis' Dora's Sugar Cookies

Mrs. Dora of Dodge City fame is said to have come from Boston's Beacon Street.

| 1 | cup butter |
| 1 | cup confectioners sugar |
| 1 | cup granulated sugar |
| 2 | eggs |
| 1 | cup oil |
| 2 | teaspoons vanilla |
| 1 | teaspoon baking soda |
| 1 | teaspoon cream of tartar |
| 1/2 | teaspoon salt |
| 5 | cups flour |
| | Granulated sugar for dipping |

In medium bowl, cream butter with confectioners sugar and granulated sugar. Beat in eggs until smooth. Slowly stir in oil, vanilla, baking soda, cream of tartar, salt and flour. Chill for easy handling. Shape into walnut-size balls. Dip in sugar. Place on baking sheet and press down. Bake in preheated oven at 350 degrees for 10-12 minutes. Makes about 4 dozen cookies.

"As I was a-walkin' one mornin' for pleasure,
I spied a young cow puncher ridin' alone,
His hat was throwed back and
                    his spurs was a-jinglin',
As he approached me a-singin' this song.

Whoopee ti yi yo, git along, little dogies,
It's your misfortune and none of my own,
Whoopie ti yi yo, git along, little dogies,
For you know Wyoming will be your new home

Some fellows goes up the trail for pleasure,
But that's where they've got it
                    most awfully wrong,
For you haven't an idea the trouble they give us,
As we go a-drivin' them dogies along."

# Bread Pudding

| | |
|---|---|
| 3 | cups bread cubes |
| 4 | cups hot milk |
| 1/2 | cup sugar |
| 3 | eggs, beaten |
| 4 | tablespoons margarine, melted |
| 1/2 | teaspoon salt |
| 1 | teaspoon vanilla |
| 3/4 | cup raisins |
| 1/4 | teaspoon nutmeg |
| 1/4 | teaspoon cinnamon |

Add bread cubes to hot milk; set aside to cool. Add remaining ingredients. Pour into buttered pan. Place pan with pudding into larger pan of hot water. Bake for 1 hour at 350 degrees. Serve warm with Whisky Hard Sauce.

# Whisky Hard Sauce:

| | |
|---|---|
| 1-1/2 | cup confectioners sugar |
| 2 | tablespoons butter, softened |
| 1 | tablespoon whisky |

Stir together and let rest a few hours to blend flavors. If too thick, add a few drops of milk. Serve over bread pudding.

# Fruit Leather

| | |
|---|---|
| 5 | cups fruit pulp |
| 1/2 | cup sugar |
| 1 | teaspoon lemon juice |

Peel, slice and pit fruit. Put fruit into a large saucepan and add sugar. Bring mixture to a boil, stirring until sugar is dissolved. Pour mixture into a blender or food processor and puree until smooth. Cool until lukewarm. Spread puree about 1/8 inch thick on plastic wrap on 2 large baking sheets. (A 12x15 inch baking sheet will hold about 3 cups puree).

Dry in direct sunlight 10 to 12 hours, or until leathery and chewy. If not dry at the end of the day, bring inside to finish. When dry and still warm from he sun, roll up the leather in the plastic wrap and seal tightly. Leather will keep at room temperature about 1 month, or in the refrigerator for 4 months, or in the freezer, for one year. (Oven Drying: Preheat oven to 200 degrees. Set baking sheets on a low oven rack and bake overnight or until leather is dry and chewy.)

# Texas Chocolate Sheet Cake

| | |
|---|---|
| 2 | cups all-purpose flour |
| 2 | cups sugar |
| 2 | eggs, beaten |
| 3/4 | cup sour cream |
| 1 | teaspoon salt |
| 1 | teaspoon baking soda |
| 1 | cup butter or margarine |
| 1 | cup water |
| 4 | heaping tablespoons cocoa |

In a bowl, mix together flour, sugar, eggs, sour cream, salt and baking soda. Set aside. In a saucepan, bring butter, water and cocoa to a boil. Remove from heat. Cool. Stir into flour mixture and beat with electric mixer at medium speed until smooth. Pour into a greased 15x10x1 inch jelly roll pan. Bake at 350 degrees for 20 to 22 minutes, or until cake tests done. Remove from oven; cool for 15 to 20 minutes. Spread with chocolate frosting.

# Chocolate Frosting

| | |
|---|---|
| 4-1/2 | cups confectioners sugar |
| 1 | teaspoon vanilla |
| 1/2 | cup butter |
| 1/4 | cup milk |
| 4 | tablespoons cocoa |
| 1 | cup chopped walnuts |

In a bowl, mix together confectioners sugar and vanilla and set aside. In a saucepan, combine butter, milk and cocoa. Bring to a boil. Remove from heat and add to sugar and vanilla. Mix well with electric mixer at medium speed, then stir in walnuts and spread over warm cake.

*"Oh, the quickly faded glory*
*Of the cowboy's brief, brief story!*
*How the old range beckons vainly in the*
*sunshine and the rain!*
*From"The Cow-Puncher's Elegy"*
by Arthur Chapman

# Pound Cake

| | |
|---|---|
| 1 | pound (2 cups) butter |
| 1 | pound (2-1/4 cups) sugar |
| 9 | eggs |
| 4 | cups sifted cake flour |
| 1 | tablespoon grated lemon rind |
| 1 | tablespoon lemon juice |

Cream butter and sugar until very light and creamy. Beat in eggs, one at a time, beating well after each addition. Gradually add flour, blending thoroughly. Add lemon rind and juice. Bake in two greased, wax paper-lined 9" by 5" pans at 350 degrees for 1 hour and 15 minutes. Frost, glaze or leave plain. Slice thin to serve. Yields 2 loaf cakes.

# Texas Pecan Pie

| | |
|---|---|
| 1 | 8 inch pastry shell |
| 3 | eggs |
| 1/2 | cup light corn syrup |
| 1 | cup sugar, white or brown |
| | Dash of salt |
| 1 | teaspoon vanilla |
| 1 | cup chopped pecans |
| | Pecan halves for garnish |

Beat eggs until frothy. Add sugar, corn syrup, salt, vanilla and pecans. Mix well. Pour into pie shell. Arrange pecans on top. Bake in hot oven, 400 degrees, for 10 minutes. Lower temperature to 350 degrees and bake 30 minutes longer or until almost firm at center. Cool. Serves 6.

# Manflo's Apple Molasses Cake

| | |
|---|---|
| 1 | cup dried apples |
| 1 | cup butter |
| 1 | cup sugar |
| 3 | eggs |
| 1 | teaspoon baking soda |
| 1 | cup molasses |
| 3 | cups flour |
| 1 | teaspoon ginger |
| 1/4 | teaspoon nutmeg |
| 1/4 | teaspoon ground cloves |
| 1 | cup milk |

Place apples in cool water overnight. Cream butter and sugar; beat in eggs. Add soda to molasses. Sift dry ingredients together. Alternately add milk, molasses and dry ingredients to butter, sugar and egg mixture. Stir in apples just enough to cover. Scoop into a large loaf pan and bake at 350 degrees for 45 minutes. If cooking on the trail, use a 14 inch Dutch oven and cook with coals on bottom and top for 45 minutes to 1 hour, or until a tooth pick inserted in center comes out clean. Serves 12.